Ancient Spellbook of Witchcraft and Old Customs

Susanne Klimt

Ancient Spellbook of Witchcraft and Old Customs

Bibliografische Information der Deutschen Nationalbibliothek:
Die Deutsche Nationalbibliothek verzeichnet diese Publikation in der
Deutschen Nationalbibliografie; detaillierte bibliografische Daten sind
im Internet über http://dnb.dnb.de abrufbar.

TWENTYSIX
Eine Marke der Books on Demand GmbH

© 2021 Susanne Klimt

Herstellung und Verlag:
BoD – Books on Demand, Norderstedt

ISBN: 9783740784126

Illustration: Anna Babic

Table of Contents

Dear Readers,

May I introduce myself to you?

My name is Susanne Klimt. I am a clairvoyant and white witch for more than 35 years.

Would you like to follow me to my World of Witchcraft? You are very welcome!

There are lots of wonderful old traditions and rituals to help yourself in case of various problems and to assist you to be a happy person again after a life crisis.

They will bring back vitality, energetic protection, love and success.

White magic is a wonderful way, to help yourself or other people. Witchcraft and its customs are practiced since ancient times. It is an enchanted way to follow the path of our ancestors, how to live in harmony with Mother Nature according to the laws of the universe.

"An Ye Harm None, Do What Ye Will"

That means you can do what you want, but don`t harm someone!

I wish you a lot of success with this little book of ancient magic!

Be blessed!

Yours truly

Susanne Klimt

Rituals and magic Spells for Love and Fertility

The goddess and the triple moon

Since ancient times the moon is a symbol for various things in magic, in ritual work, in everyday life and in the herb garden. Much attention is given to the phases of the moon, to help determine if it is a good time to plant something, or if it is better to weed the garden. Moon wood built houses are more stable, and in the kitchen, meals turn out better if the moon has the right position.

Did you know that the moon reflects the sign of the Goddess in us? It is no coincidence that the moon is connected with femininity. Also in Wicca cults, the religion of witches, the identification sign is called the triple moon. The waxing moon, full moon, or waning moon stands symbolically for the young girl, the mature woman, and for the wise woman. These different phases of life all have a special time quality and if they are accepted by the people, it will greatly enrich our life and knowledge.

Like everything in nature, which germinates, blossoms, fruits, and slowly withers away, so does the moon. If we adjust to this cycle, we will feel great, but if we work against it, we will recognize that we cannot slow it down. We are all part of nature, and its laws, and we cannot bypass them.

Why is this trinity so important and what is the sense of it all?

If we take a close look, then we can see that this threefold Goddess is in every woman. It is not the point of getting older and matured, but the attributes which lay in us. Sometimes we are back to that little girl, and other times we are the mature vamp with life experience.

Even if we look young, we can feel very old. Women live according to the moon, and its vibrations. Every different phase of the moon makes us aware of it. Just as the moon has its cycles, so the woman has her monthly cycles.

Therefore, awaken that Goddess within you! Let the femininity take over!

You will need:

- A handful of white blossoms, like Jasmine,
- A small Moonstone,
- Three small, light Flintstones,
- One big bowl,
- Sufficient water to fill the bowl,
- One big white Alter candle,
- Some silver glitter, or silver stars,
- Aroma, Ylang Ylang oil,
- Fragrance lamp and a candle to fit it,
- Matches

The best time for this ritual is a night with a bright, full moon.

You will need a quiet place in your home, or better yet, outside in the open.

Put the big white candle and the Moonstone into the bowl and fill it up to one third with the water. Now scatter the blossoms around the bowl in a circle. Then put the Ylang-Ylang oil into the fragrance lamp, and light the candle underneath it. Keep the three Flintstones and the glitter handy beside the bowl.

If you are performing the ritual outdoors, face the moon, and cross your arms in front of your chest, then speak the following spell:

"Great Goddess of the Moon, since the first hour of my life, you shine upon my pasture, you are with me every day and every night. You stimulate me with feminine and intuition. You have numerous names, yet always are one. Fill me up with your light, and let me feel your presence in my heart."

Now open your arms, and take the first Flintstone, and put it into the bowl, then speak the following words:

"As a symbol for the young virgin, I put this stone into the bowl of the Goddess of the Moon!"

Then take the second stone, and place it into the bowl and say:

"As a sign of a mature woman, I put this stone into the holy bowl!"

Now take the last one and place it into the bowl, then say:

"To honour the old woman, I add on the last stone!"

Now take the glitter and let it trickle slowly into the bowl and speak the following words:

"Like the sparkling of the stars, may I discover the Goddess within me by your force and glory! I light up this light (light the candle) so that all this may be! So be it, so be it, so be it! I thank you, lovely Goddess of the Moon, for your assistance, and take in your good energies!"

Remain with outspreaded arms in the moon light and admit the feelings, because at that moment, when you feel the Goddess, some blockades will dissolve.

From now on, be all woman! This change within you will also be noticed by your surroundings, and don`t be astonished, if men suddenly make more compliments than ever before!

The magic ring of love

A ring is a very important symbol in traditional white magic. It has its own mystical power. In relationships it's a sign of eternity. A lot of very famous tales are surrounding magical rings since hundreds of years. For example in Tolkiens wonderful book named "Lord of the rings" it is a jewelry with a powerful magic!

Also a very old legend is told in Germany. A magical ring made by Alberich, king of the fairies and dwarfs, is still in the deepness of the river Rhine. Whenever someone will find it, he can be the king of the world! The creepiest rings of witchcraft I have ever seen are made from human bones.

Thank heaven materials like that are not being used in white magic! According to the laws of the universe most of the rings are made of noble metal, and in magical practice metal can be charged.

All kind of wishes like richness, health, success or friendship can be obtained with a magical ring. Various wishes are possible. The most well-known wish associated with a ring is Partnership.

One of the most enchanted rings in the world is the well-known Irish Claddagh. It is a pure Symbol of love and it keeps its good vibrations up till today. It was getting so famous, that it is still used as a wedding ring all over the world. Love is the greatest power we have and real love is a language the whole world understands!

So I will show you an old ritual how to load a magical ring to attract a new love, or to stabilize a Partnership. Work on waxing moon, preferably close to the full moon and if possible on a Friday, which is sacred to the Venus.

You will need:

- 1 silver or golden ring
- Thread
- A handful of rose petals
- Frankincense, incense burner and charcoal
- 1 red candle, candleholder, matches

It is very important, first to consider which desire should be fulfilled with this ritual! If you have made you decision light up the charcoal and put it in the incense burner.

After a while the charcoal will turn grey. It is the right time to put a small portion frankincense on top. Light the candle and sprinkle the rose petals in a circle on the table.

Put the thread through the ring and sway it seven times through the smoke. It will clean it from negative energies. Now you are going to charge the ring with a magical spell!

Just sit comfortably upright and relaxed, down with both feet on the ground. Take the ring between the palms of your hands and close your eyes. Imagine how golden and pink light flows into the ring between your hands. Formulate your request and speak the following incantation:

"With the power of the universe I consecrate this ring,

to attract always love in my being!

Let the right one quickly be at my side,

and fill me with the sense of great delight!

A faithful man/woman with true love,

a beautiful soul and peaceful heart.

Oh holy Venus I invoke you,

to make my wish of love come true!

So shall it be!"

Please keep this picture for a few minutes more, and imagine how the ring turns golden and pink coloured. Your wish will literally get burn into the ring.

From now on the magical ring will be your favourite piece of Jewelry! Whenever you want to activate the love energy again, you just have to turn the ring on your finger to the left, and you will feel the warmth of this magical item. It will be your personal good luck and love charm!

Bake your perfect partner!

Long time ago, my dear grandmother said to me: "If you want to find your perfect partner, the man who is meant for you, you will have to bake him!" However, how should you "bake" a man and what has that to do with serious and respectable magic work? You won't believe it, but it has a lot to do with it!

If we have a look at the traditional rituals with regard to baked goods, we will see that many old customs and traditions still exist today. Bread, which is made of grain, is always associated with Demeter, the "Earth Mother"

You will find bread as a sacrificial offering on every altar. In former times, dough was used to create figures in order to put a request to the gods. Very often, bread of different shapes and also cakes are used for ritual requests. You will definitely know the Easter wreath. Before Easter, people bake that white bread which is woven of three ropes of dough, the symbols of trinity.

In the middle of the wreath, they put a red-coloured boiled egg, the symbol of fertility and rebirth. If you eat it, you will internalise the blessing of the universe. Through this blessing, fertility shall be guaranteed for the family as well as for the farming. According to an old belief, a small piece will have to be kept in the house for one year so that the good spirit will always be in the house.

You see, baking is in accord with magic!

But how can you "bake" your perfect partner by means of white magic?

You need the following items and ingredients:

- Quick bread mix for a white bread and the necessary ingredients (if you want, you can also use your own recipe)
- 1 white candle
- 2 fully dyed red candles
- vanilla sugar
- cinnamon powder
- raisins (for the eyes)
- petals of red roses
- rose water
- Styrax incense, charcoal and censer

Start the ritual on a Saturday evening. Prepare the bread dough for baking, light the charcoal, wait until it is glowing and put the Styrax on top.

Consecrate the candles using the rose water. Now light the white candle first. Take the dough and imagine what your perfect partner should look like. While you are forming the dough, say the following spell:

"Come to me elements,
be with me today,
help to bake my perfect partner
to join me on my way.

Please send him to me,
let him be at my side,
because I do not want
to be alone in my life.

Come to me my love
with passion and affection,
against negative influence
I add cinnamon's protection.

Let him be faithful,
honest and true,
now I add the vanilla,
which will bring temptation, too.

Bring me the perfect partner,
the best person of all,
an honest and true man,
not too tall and not too small.

Remove all obstacles
from my path to him.
I wait for the man to go with
through thick and through thin.

All elements come to me,
attend at my magic ritual
and help me to find him,
the best partner of all!
So shall it be, so shall it be, so shall it be!"

While you are kneading and forming the dough, imagine what your perfect partner should look like. The more you think of him, the more positive energies will be put into the dough. Let your imagination run wild! That will give power to the ritual.

Now take the red candles and light them at the white candle. Put the bread figure into the oven and while the "man" is baking, scatter a handful of rose petals in front of the candles.

As soon as the bread figure is ready, let it cool down and put it on the petals in front of the burning candles. Wait until the candles have burnt down completely.

The baked figure should stay on the rose petals until the perfect man has found his way to you. You can eat a tiny little piece of the bread so that you will internalise your request and you will carry the good vibrations of this ritual with you. That will automatically attract the "Man of your Dreams".

I heartily wish you that you will meet the person who is meant for you as soon as possible and that you will live a happy life with him, full of harmony, good health and love!

Potion of Love

In summertime cool drinks and fresh fruits are very tasty. It is a good opportunity to create some love potions!

Since ancient times there are a lot of recipes and magic spells for special occasions. In witchcraft such magical potions are mostly brewed in a three legged cauldron. One of the most famous legends about a magical cauldron is the tale of Cerridwen - the welsh Goddess of the moon. Her cauldron was warmed by nine young maidens with their breath! She created a special enchanted brew for her three sons to give them special skills. The magical brew had to simmer for three years. Those three years where associated with inspiration, knowledge and wisdom. It symbolizes the long way to learn the complex issues in witchcraft.

Magical brews are made for enlightment of our spiritual thinking. It teaches us how to transform different ingredients to a powerful tool or healing potion. In witchcraft there are also known a lot of elixirs which can open the doors to the underworld. Witches created them to get more consciousness about the metaphysical and spiritual being. Sometimes these dangerous elixirs have been very poisonously! They have taken plants like foxglove, elder, toadstool or deadly nightshade to get in contact with the creatures between the worlds. It is not suggestible to brew this kind of potions, because they can cause serious health issues or death! Since thousands of years the cauldron symbolizes the source of very effective potions for all kind of purposes.

A real witch is not able to work properly without her cauldron, because it is one of the most important tools for enchanting. A white witch and her cauldron belong together like a hairdresser and its scissors or a Blacksmith with its forge. In white magic we don`t need piousness ingredients anymore. Modern witches don`t want to harm their self or other people. That is the reason why, I want to show you a modern and very effective ritual to make your partnership fulfilled with love, passion and desire.

How does it work? Here we go!

You will need:

- 1 pomegranate
- 1 fresh fig
- 1 pinch of chili powder
- 1 pinch of cinnamon
- half a teaspoon of fresh Ginger
- 2 teaspoons full of honey
- 2 fresh red-leaved roses (please select untreated plants)
- 1 bottle of red wine
- A sieve, a pot and a carafe

Open the Pomegranate and strain the Berries through the sieve. Cut the Fig into small pieces and combine the ingredient together with the Cinnamon, Chili, Ginger and honey into the Pomegranate juice. Just heat the red wine in a pan and simmer it. Do not boil! Give all the ingredients in the warm red wine and whilst stirring the magical brew imagine how you and the woman / man of your heart are melting together and having a good time full with love and desire! The more you can visualize, the greater is the success! Let the magical brew cool down and pick the blossom petals from the roses. When the magic brew is cooled down fill it in a carafe. Sprinkle the leaves upon the love brew. Take the carafe in your hands, close your eyes and speak the following spell:

"Lovely Aphrodite please fill this brew,

With love, desire and magic too!

Show the Woman/man the way to my heart,

Let us be like each other's part!

In love, health and happiness,

This magical brew will help me yet!

So be it, so be it, so be it!"

Take the carafe and kiss the seam with your mouth. That is the way how your own energy will flow in every glass of brew you fill in. Of course you need a romantic atmosphere too! You can decorate your room delightly with rose petals, candlelight and fill an incense burner with Styrax, Sandalwood or Jasmine. Drink the white magic love potion together with the woman/man of your heart. It`s made for you! Just try it and you will feel the difference!

I wish you a lot of success with this white magic love potion and summer nights full with love and desire!

Love and Fertility

Hare in the moon

"In the black furror of a field

I saw an old witch-hare this night;

And she cocked a lissome ear,

And she eyed the moon so bright,

And she nibbled of the green;

And I whispered "Whsst! witch-hare,"

Away like a ghostie o'er the field

She fled, and left the moonlight there."

(Poem by Walter de la Mare)

Have you ever seen a hare in the moon? Did you know that hares are very closely connected to white magic? Come with me in my world of witchcraft. I will explain to you how to use the power of white magic to get love, fertility and blessed with children.

A lot of goddesses are associated with the hare. Freya, Aphrodite, Holda, Hectate, Cerridwen or Ostara they all represent love, beauty and fertility. All of them are closely connected with the myths of the hare. In old pictures or on carvings in stone or wood, a hare is always present as a symbol of goddesses. These goddesses are also said to take the shape of a hare at each full moon. In witchcraft the moon gazing hare has significant magical symbolism. It is natural that witches love Mother Nature and are excellent interpreter of the seasons. In March and April the hares are a signal for the upcoming springtime. Normally these are nocturne creatures, but in awakening of nature they are seen on the fields at any time of the day.

"Mad as a March hare!" is a very popular phrase and there stands reason behind the old saying. "Springtime is the beginning of their mating season. The males will be seen acting strangely and appear quite "mad" in their antics, especially if rebuffed by a female. He doesn't realize that he is making a fool of himself by boxing and jumping around. Because of the old tales it is no surprise why hares are a little bit scary for some men!

In ancient believe it is told that old women and witches could transform into a hare or rabbit. The roman commander Julius Caesar reported on his Gallic crusades that the Celtic tribes had forbidden the eating of a hare. In ancient Ireland a person who ate a hare was indicted to eat his grandma or wife! In Pagan believe no human should harm a hare or rabbit because every hare is a transformed goddess!

The most beautiful sign of a hare is seen in a clear Easter night. According to an old Asian legend, at full moon you can see the silhouette of a hare. The legend goes like this: A few thousand years ago the animals of the forest decided to do charity. An old poor beggar was sitting on their way. He was full of hunger and so they decided to get him some food. The otter has caught some fish, wolves brought milk, eggs and chicken and the monkeys carried vegetables, fruits and nuts to him.

Of all the animals, only the hare couldn't bring him anything to eat. The hare got so sad about this because he wanted to help too. Full of sadness he lit a fire and jumped into the flames to serve as a meal for the beggar. The old man was so surprised that a creature of the universe was giving his live for him in act of charity that he took the hare out of the fire and rescued him. No harm was done to the hare because the old man wasn't a beggar. His name was Sakka – King of the gods! So as a symbol of his act of charity he placed an eternal picture of the hare in the moon.

This old legend tells us how important the status of a hare is seen all over the world! There are many more wonderful stories about the animal with the long ears and fluffy tail, but let us return to the meaning of hares in witchcraft. It is no wonder rabbits and hares have often been witches' familiars, for hares are said to be wanderers between the worlds. In every case the hare is shown to be a symbol of the goddesses, love, rebirthing and fertility. I would like to explain an old white magic ritual for fertility and partnership.

You will need:

- 1 green candle, candleholder, matches
- Yellow ribbon
- 1 egg
- 1 sheet of green paper, 1 black pencil, a small shovel

Start on the Saturday night before Easter. Look out for a quiet place and create a harmonic atmosphere. Then light the candle. Draw a hare on the sheet of paper. Don't worry- it is not expected that you can paint like the famous Picasso or Rembrandt!

When you have finished your picture of the hare, take the egg and wrap it into the paper. To keep it close together, tie the yellow ribbon around the little parcel. After you have done that hold the fertility package in your hands while you are looking up to the moon. Visualize your wish to be blessed with children and speak the following spell:

"Hare, hare bring me the three,

A man, love and fertility!

Your face in the moon is shining on me,

please bless me with children,

So shall it be!"

Bury the magical hare package in a small pit nearby an old oak. This is needed because in white magic we use the element earth to mani-fest your spell. Stay at your magic place and let the moonlight shine on you till the candle has burn down.

If you meet some hares on your way home you can be sure, that the universe has heard your magic spell!

I wish you a lot of success with this old hare ritual and may many healthy children be your own!

Goddess Freya`s ritual of Fertility

Children are a divine gift and the future of mother earth! They give us joy and sometimes even awake the child within us, so that some dad's go with a glow in their eyes and play with the new electric train. One of the happiest moments in a young mother's life is when her child calls her "mummy" for the first time.

Not every couple though is granted the wish for a child right away. In a case like that people in the olden days, and even today, would go to a white witch to get advice. These were usually mid-wifes and substitutes for a gynecol-ogist.

There are countless white magical rituals to help being blessed with children. Some of them I would like to introduce to you!

Numerous Goddesses can help making a wish for a child come true.

Aphrodite is the Greek Goddess of love, or Venus, whom the an-cient romans gave the mother roll, Ishtar of the Babylonians or Astarte of Syria, just to name a few, they all supported fertility.

In northern parts it is Freya of the Celts who was worshiped in dif-ferent ceremonies in order to become pregnant. To support that wish, everything that could be associated with the womb was used in ritual ways. Things like apples, walnuts, little bags, female figures made of stone or wood, pits of peaches, eggs and much more.

Some traditions were held over into Christianity. Little dolls made of wax would be brought into church to be blessed with children. Prior to Christianity people would also make these little figures from clay which were symbols of femininity.

These were brought to the alter or other powerful places, to pray for support. Women brought little offerings to make the Goddesses friendly, for instance apples, because it was the food of Gods or some wine made from honey called "Met".

Even holy wells were often mentioned concerning the wish for children. To drink a bit of the water and some taken home was to bring the desired fertility. Whoever doesn't want to go out, she can do a few things at home. For example lay a few leaves of pewter grass underneath your bed; it's supposed to bring quick results!

Other traditions say that a mirror put upside down underneath your bed works the same way. However, do not remove the mirror again, until the child is born! All dirt-obsessed housewives should spare that spot, because the dirt can be removed later.

A lovely advice I got from a lady, which I spoke to the other day, is that in her younger day's young couples were given the advice to put a cube of sugar onto the windowsill ! When I asked her, why that? She answered, well it's simple, when the stork, who brings the babies, comes and see's the sugar, he is delighted, eats the goody and a few months later he brings the baby! The lady has two children, so apparently the strategy worked. I found this a very lovely story and wanted you to participate in it.

Dear readers, I want to tell you something that you can do in matters of white magic, to support your child wish. Of course you should always consult a doctor before to make sure, that there is no sickness or lack of hormones. If all is well, you can go ahead with a little bit of white magic.

Take a walnut and open it carefully, so that you have two halves in good condition, put some cotton in them, form a doll from wax and place it inside. Then put as many apple pips (seeds) into it as you want children. After that join the nutshells back together and seal it with warm wax.

Now take the nut in both hands, close your eyes and speak the following words:

"Dear universe I beg of you,

grant me blessing of children!

As many children as there are apple pips (seeds) within this nut,

Goddess Freya please support me!

May they be healthy and blessed with love,

that they may always be on the sunny side of life!

With the power of the universe,

please send me fertility right now!

So be it, so be it, so be it!"

Now visualise how this little walnut is being loaded with a lot of energy and put it into your bedroom. It is an ancient rule that says this wish will be granted within seven months.

Magic or not, please don't forget your partner! Without him nothing will work! There is one little magic thing you can do to seduce him: Take a little bit of parsley, lovage or celery and mix it in his supper. These are aphrodisiacs since God knows when, and will awake in him a desire for Eroticism. With this and a bit of romantic you should be able to persuade your loved one.

Keep that little nut hidden in a secret place in your bedroom until all the children have been born and are well off.

I wish you from the bottom of my heart that your wishes for healthy children come true!

Lucky charms and wishes

Inner Balance with Peppermint

Nowadays it is hard to find inner harmony and balance. However, there is something that we can do to meet the challenges of life! How does that work? I will show you a little ritual which you can easily do by yourselves. First of all, I would like to tell you something about the plant which we need as an item for that ritual!

One of the best known magic herbs is "Mentha Piperita", also called "peppermint". That very popular medicinal plant, which had already been known in former times, has its mythological origin in the world of gods of ancient Greece.

Peppermint is closely associated with Mintha. She was the lover of Hades, the god of the underworld. When his wife Persephone learnt of that, she tore Mintha to shreds and scattered them on earth. Nobody should see the beauty of the nymph so that she could not bewitch men any more.

According to the legend, peppermint grew from those pieces and heavenly justice made peppermint into a plant with the most bewitching smells of those times. Whenever you break a sprig, you will immediately smell that lovely and refreshing fragrance. This way, Mintha's attractive charisma remained preserved by that lovely smell.

In ancient Egypt, they already knew the fantastic effects of the essential oils of that plant. They were burial objects in order to guard the dead bodies from evil spirits during their afterlife.

In classical Rome, they already used the refreshing effect of that plant in case of headache and problems with the throat, ears and nose. They said that rubbing the dining table with fresh leaves of the peppermint, would stimulate the appetite.

In the bible, the peppermint is described as a plant which performs miracles. For that reason, its fragrance is highly appreciated in churches. Peppermint was a must in every household even before the smelling salts were used.

Nowadays, we use peppermint mainly as tea in case of stomach upset, diarrhoea and nausea. It has a sedative effect and is also used for bad colds. If you put the oil of the peppermint into an aromatherapy lamp, it will refresh the mind. Lavender and fir needles put into a censer will clean rooms and will protect from negative energies.

The name "peppermint" was created by John Ray, a British natural scientist, who found big quantities of that nicely smelling plant in a garden approx. 400 years ago. As the peppermint had a rather hot taste, he called it "peppermint".

If you plant it in your garden, it will be a good pesticide, but will also attract useful insects like bees and bumblebees. If you plant it into bigger flower pots, it will look nice even on your balcony.

For magic meditation, the peppermint leaves must be dried. The best way to do this is to hang up the sprigs head down and to pick the peppermint leaves once they are dry.

In addition, you need the following items:

- Dried lavender blooms
- 1 censer and charcoal
- 1 small white bag
- 1 white and 1 green fully dyed candle
- and a candle-holder

Start that little ritual on a Sunday morning. If the weather is nice, celebrate that ritual in the open countryside. Nature gives power to us and combines the different elements!

Light the candles and also the charcoal in the censer. As soon as the charcoal is glowing, put some lavender blooms and peppermint leaves on top. Close your eyes and imagine that a cloudy sky slowly brightens up and the grey sky becomes blue.

Imagine that some of the sun's rays gently touch your face as on a beautiful day in spring. Visualise golden sunlight and let it flow through your body. Pause for a few minutes and feel the inner peace.

After that, take the little bag and while you are filling in the peppermint leaves and the lavender blooms, say the following spell:

"I will fill this little bag,

so innocent and white,

with the wonderful herbs

and the sun's warm light.

Let me rely on myself,

give power to me!

Oh, wonderful blossoms,

give me inner harmony!

Create good vibrations,

give me help and hope!

Lead me through my life

and cure my soul!

I would like to be happy.

Oh universe attend to me!

Give me hope and support

and much new energy!

I gladly accept joy

and whenever it is time,

I will give it to somebody

and a little bit of sunshine.

I will catch the sun's rays

and will fill the bag with those.

I will now take it with me

to my home and my house.

So shall it be, so shall it be, so shall it be!"

This little bag will now contain the power of the herbs and of that ritual. Put it under your pillow during the night and you will feel that your dreams will become better and you will get new energy while you are sleeping.

Sometimes it is so easy to feel good!

Magical clover charm

In springtime Mother Nature is slowly awakening to new life. The favorite colour of this month is green because everywhere the trees in the forest are getting green again and spring flowers start to bloom. It`s only natural that a lot of magical rituals are connected to this color. On St. Patrick`s Day in Ireland superstition and pagan customs revolve all around this color. The patron of Ireland disinfested the country of a snake worriment, armed only with a stick. He did a lot of other miracles too.

In ancient times there were no snakes on the emerald island but it must rather be regarded symbolically, because in Christian believe snakes are a symbol of the evil. So the holy St. Patrick fought against it! He made the Christian believe very popular all over the country because he preached to the people, that a shamrock (clover leaf) is a symbol for the holy trinity. The God Father, the Son and the Holy Spirit. He wanted to show that God is omnipresent, because there are a lot of shamrocks covering the isle! In witches believe a shamrock is also a sign for goddesses! It is a trinity called "Maiden, Mother and Crone"

On St. Patrick`s Day all Irish woman and men are wearing a nosegay of shamrocks on their dress. In pagan believe the color green is associated with health and good fortune. So on this spectacular day everyone wears only green clothing. If someone doesn't accept this dress code, I won't tell him to go outside! It is an old custom that other people who are celebrating St. Patrick's Day would tickle him! On this day everything seems to be colored green. The food, the beer, houses and also the rivers are dyed with eco- friendly green color. It is a real famous festival!

The old Irish legends are telling also about a little green man who lives deep in the forest. It is the Leprechaun- an always stressed shoemaker of the fairies and trolls. In thousands of years they earned a lot of gold with their job. They hide their treasures at secret places. Sometimes when a wandering human hears the hammering sound of the shoemaker, he finds the house of the Leprechaun too! The legend tells that at the end of the rainbow the trolls placed a pot of gold! A human who finds the pot should be careful! Fairy and troll gold won't keep and after a few seconds it turns into stone, ash or earth! So if you ever meet a Leprechaun at his work you should better help him than ask for gold!

Giving is worth more than taking! This is the guiding principle of the universe. If you follow these cosmic laws the Leprechaun will reward you with a little golden gift!

Witchcraft is very close connected to nature and the old fairy tales. That's the reason why the color green is very important in white magic too. Witches associate the color green with joy, hope, eternal life and success! Green tells us always a "Yes"! Green has a positive power and for mankind it symbolizes "I can! " Think about the traffic lights, because you can drive or walk when the lights turn green.

Or just take a look at your phone, even as usual the answer key has a green colour. Emergency exits have green signs, and most school boards are kept in dark green, to inspire the pupils to learn. Advertising experts are specialized to find the right shade of green to increase the success of a product. I would like to show you a small Irish ritual, which quite excellent fits into the upcoming spring after a long winter!

You will need:

- 1 small bunch of shamrocks
- 1 green candle
- Mint oil
- 1 green ribbon
- 1 book, some paper towels or blotting paper

Cast this spell on the 17th of March – on St. Patrick`s Day. Get out into nature and pick up some clover including the stems along the way. Return to your home and consecrate the candle with the mint oil. Now tie the clover leaves to a small bunch. Take the tiny little bouquet in your hands while casting following spell:

"Oh holy St. Patrick,

In honour to you,

I keep these shamrocks,

In believing of you!

The shamrock promises me,

Hope, luck and health,

A wonderful year fulfilled with wealth!

So mote it be!"

Imagine how green light energy flows through your hands and charge the nosegay with positive energy. Now put it gently between some blotting paper. Place it between the pages of the book. After just two weeks, take the dried leaves out from the book and put it in a place where you are spending most time of the day.

It looks very pretty if you place the lucky charm under glass in a small picture frame. You can also give this magical clover as a present to the people of your heart! This spell keeps exactly one year till the next Saint Patrick's Day!

I wish you a great springtime and a lot of joy with the white magic ritual in honor of St. Patrick! May millions of clovers cover your way!

Key to fortune

What does a magician mean when he speaks about a secret key? Often spoken off, but most people don't know the meaning of this mysterious tool.

The meaning of this symbol is closely connected to our everyday life. Every time we have something very precious or private, that we don't want others to see, we lock it away and keep a close eye on the key and we decide, who shall have access to it and who not.

There are also a lot of fateful doors in our life! Sometimes we have to lock up one of those doors in order to find another one to open!

Also, we have magical keywords in form of a puzzle, so no one can misuse it. Only insiders know this coded language. Even in fairy tales we have magic code words, like "Abracadabra".

Words can, like keys, open doors to the world beyond and activate frequencies which are very powerful! These symbols, which look like small simple signs, are often unnoticed by people, which can be used for certain intentions. For example a spiral can open or close something.

Pentagrams or Pentacles can protect or appeal to the elements. The signet of Salomon, the hexagonal star, stands for communication with spirits and the four elements.

In this spectacular sign you can see two triangles. The triangle, and this is a fact, is one of the most powerful keys in magic! It is mentioned in almost every culture and religion and stands for the holy trinity. There would be a lot more to mention, but let us look to a small little

36

ritual, which you can celebrate yourself in order to get an individual magic key.

For the "Key to Fortune" you need the following utensils:

- 1 little key (new and unused)
- 1 violet candle
- 1 incense burner and charcoal
- 1 small bowl
- Frankincense mix from amber, angelica root and dried orange peel
- 1 golden ribbon
- 1 small green tablecloth.

Start this ritual on a Tuesday evening. Light up the charcoal and put some incense on it. After that put the bowl on the green tablecloth and thread the ribbon through the key. Now light the candle and swing the key through the smoke in order to clean it.

Than imagine for which door in your life you want to use this key because there are many ways of employment! For example:

- to attract fortune in your life
- being protected against negative energies
- open a heart of a beloved person
- success in business
- intensify your spirituality

Whatever you imagine, it is important that you don't harm anyone with your wish and that you act according to the laws of the Universe.

If you are certain, what you want the key for, hold it in your hand tightly, imagine now, how pure energy and light develops in your hands. You will even be able to feel the warmth.

Visualize your wish and say the following spell:

"Key to fortune, I consecrate you,

you shall be expedient to me!

Open new doors quickly,

The right – and bright ones only!

Let me find my personal new ways,

with health and perfect satisfaction.

My magic key, you fit into the locks of my life,

and you accompany me on all my ways.

From now on you only belong to me

and you will protect me against dark energies.

So be it, so be it, so be it!"

After you kept the key for a moment in your hands, put it around your neck or in your pocket. Pay attention to the key in critical situations, or when you have to make decisions, the key will get warm if you are on the right way!

Also if the key wants to attract your attention to something, you will feel the warmth, so that you can find the "right door". If it stays cold, it is a definite "No".

You now have a precious magical tool, which will help you always to find the right way!

Never the less, let yourself be guided by your own intuition, because the most important key in our life is the key to heartiness!

I wish you a lot of success with this ritual and that the "Key to fortune" may always open the right door for you!

How to attract gold and money

The most significant metal in white magic is gold. It stands for riches, prosperity, healing and light full solar energy, as well as warmth, security and good thoughts. No other metal has changed the history of mankind than gold.

It is the first metal that was known by humans. All over the world, it has brought up much fascination.

Not without reason it turns up in many sagas and legends as a mysterious treasure. No wonder that alchemists of the middle age tried so hard to produce it. The so called "Stone of Wisdom", as the production of gold was called, was the highest goal of many alchemists.

Alchemists worked for hundreds of years in strange looking laboratories to get the chemical formula for making gold. Kings and Aristocrats promised them big sums of money and paid their work generously.

Unfortunately, the alchemists didn't find any such formula, but by trying, some of the best discoveries had been made, for instance-Porcelain, which is the reason it`s also called "The white gold"!

The world-famous magician and healer called Paracelsus used gold for healing and antiphlogistic procedures, and even today it is being used in hospitals against rheumatism.

Gold is a very spiritual and good material of mother earth and in white magic it is associated with wellbeing. In times like ours, where money is getting worth less and less, I show you a little ritual to attract riches and prosperity.

However, gold and money is not the most important point in our life but it comforts you, if you have a little more of it!

For this white magic ritual you need following items:

- 1 golden and one green candle
- a little bowl
- gold coloured coins, for example 1 English pound, you can also use your jewelry
- a little white tablecloth
- incense like myrrh and amber
- incense burner, charcoal, matches
- a golden ballpoint pen
- one sheet of greaseproof paper
- golden glitter
- 3 white lilies

Cast this ritual on a Tuesday evening. Spread out the white tablecloth and place the little bowl in the middle. Put the golden coins or the jewelry into it. Now light up the charcoal and after it glows put some incense on it.

Then light up the candles and write your wish with the golden pen on the paper. Please use the words "Riches", "Prosperity" "Uncorcern" "Money" "Gold" on it.

Please don't put your wishes too high, because in white magic we only wish for the things we really need! Too much riches lessens our view.

Use this ritual like a good Perfume, less is sometimes more! Now put the paper underneath the bowl. Take the lilies and knock some of the blossom powder in your hands.

After that you drape the flowers around the bowl. Then rub the pollen in your hands and add some of the glitter. Spread slowly that mixture over the bowl and cloth.

Now say the following words:

"Just like this dust in my hand,

money and gold may now come to me.

Universe I beg of you,

let prosperity be my companion now,

like I'm spreading out this gold,

bring richness in my house!

May money grow right now,

cause poverty did never let me rest,

peace shall now come to my mind,

no more worries shall I have!

Elements please support me

and make me feel free.

No more lack of money shall there be,

money shall increase like the sand on the shore at the sea!

Sunshine and gold shall now flow in,

and golden rays into my being.

Money to money and gold to gold,

so shall it be, luck please stick to me!"

Now please visualize how the gold in that little bowl becomes more and more, because this is very important that you can accept it being happening to you, visualize that you are being wrapped in golden light! At the end say out loud *"so be it, so be it, so be it!"*

Let the candles and the incense burn down to the end. After that take a bath and keep on visualizing bathing in Gold.

Please don't use this ritual only for money! You can use it also for getting positive and light full energetic belongs. Golden light is very good for our cells and makes us feel very powerful!

I wish you great success with this little white magical ritual and hope that from now on only good times are coming your way!

Magical dolls

The traditional white magic uses small dolls to attract positive vibrations and ward off negative attacks. These dolls are made for several occasions and are not to be mixed up with the voodoo dolls of the Caribbean!

These bring more harm to a person and in white magic those intentions are strictly forbidden! White witches use self-made dolls for helping humans and animals!

Since ancient times the people in Europe believe in the great power of magic dolls. For example in autumn it is a very popular tradition to place small corn dolls at the corners of the fields in order to protect them from demons.

From the straw of the wheat, the figures are braided and wrapped in red ribbons. The people imagined that a wheat demon that sees the corn dolly went away without damage to the fields believing that has been already another demon.

The witches used to place magic wishing dolls at holy places. For example at Clootie Wells because they believe that a beloved person should be healed very quickly. The Christian Church adopted this pagan custom, and therefore the believers brought modeled wax dolls, mostly with name plates in numerous churches.

Especially in the south of Germany, this ancient form of prayer is still used also today and there are still even some experts, who can do this special artwork made from wax. If there is one person for example with pain in her heart its used to hung up a small heart made from wax with her name nearby the altar of the chapel. People pray to the Lord and beg for recovery. Even small, lovely dressed dolls were brought to sacred places to pray for the health of a child.

Magical dolls are also made to protect the house against all evil! An interesting example is the "Chimney Doll". Placed high above the fireplace this magical figure keeps a close eye on the house to protect it against fire or accidents. This beautifully dressed doll, said to have a real life of its own. Like the good spirit of a house, this doll night and day is the "security man" for the whole family!

The worry dolls have their home in South America. A whole family of dolls has space in a tiny little bag! To represent each member of the family a small image is made from wool, paper, ribbons and pearls. The reason why those miniature dolls of the family are called "worry dolls" is because in the evening, when you are going to bed, you can tell them all kinds of sorrows. Overnight the sorrows will disappear. In a magical way the little worry dolls have taken away all problems and spend positive solutions for the new day.

Since hundreds of years witches prepare small dolls for people seeking advice. For health, protection or to find a new love- everything is possible. According to ancient traditions, the owner of this magical doll should take care of it. Symbolically a meal and drink should be served to it every day to keep it in a good humor.

A very important place in the history of the magical dolls is given to the roots of the mandrakes. If there is even a kind Mandrake in a family, it is stored carefully in a box. Passed on from generation to generation, it keeps its magical charisma for centuries. The Mandrake protects a house against all evil!

In witchcraft, it is custom to produce small, white magic dolls made from real bees wax. This can be formed very easily and the base material has always been bringing good luck to the holder. In pre-Christian times it was said to bring luck if someone carries three bees in a pouch to attract positive vibrations. So that is the reason why I would like to describe how to make a small magical doll which can be used in many ways!

You will need the following supplies:

- 200 grams of real bee wax
- colorful rags / wool
- 1 wooden skewer or thin knitting needle
- Rose oil

Warm the wax slightly in the sun or between your hands. Cut out the pieces of fabric scraps which will later serve as a "dress" for the doll. The hair is made of strings from wool. If the wax is warm and pliable, knead and form it into a small figure.

Just think about the person that you want to be positively protected. This can also be yourself, a loved one, a member of the family or a friend.

When the doll is fully formed sprinkle it slightly with rose oil. Now you can let your creativity run wild! Depending on whether the figure should be male or female, it is getting dressed with pants or skirt. Fix it with some glue. Let's go on with the hairstyle!

It is really easy because you take the wool and stick it with the wooden skewer or knitting needle into the wax. It will keep! Finally, you can give the doll a face. You can lightly carve the facial features very easily with a little knife or the skewer. Now it gets exciting!

Take the puppet between the palms of your hands. The wishing doll is now getting "inspired" by a white magical spell!

Speak the following words:

"I hold you now you good spirit in my hands,

I bless and ordain you with all strength and confidence,

Help whenever there is need and watch when danger threatens.

Protect (name of the person) at all times so that there will never be grief or sorrow.

So be it, so be it, so be it!"

This doll now represents the person you are wishing health, energy and love. From this moment the magical doll plays a protective role and will be useful for whom it was made. Please cherish the doll and do not expose it carelessly into a corner.

Put a few coins, a little heart or something else you like to associate with a good and pleasant life at the dolls place too. May love always surround that person at any time and may only good spirits be at his/her side. Fresh flowers and snacks, for example a piece of chocolate is representing joy and pleasure. Let your imagination run wild and please care lovingly for the magic doll at all times!

Give it a little attention every day and you will feel the positive power of white magic. Whenever we send some good energy into the world, a part of these vibrations will return to you!

Superstitions of the sea

With dreamy looks at the waves and ships, hardly anyone thinks about the seafarer, whom even today; have many traditions coming from white magic which they still treasure.

Superstition plays a big part in seafaring, because every captain knows how much power and strength the elements demand of the ship and crew. With great respect to the wind and the water, many ships will not leave port before certain rituals have taken place.

Good luck charms and other curious things to keep lady luck in their favour. All these good luck charms came from the houses of the "harbour witches", which you can find in most villages close to the sea. The superstition of fishermen and seafarers starts before they leave the harbour.

On New Year's Day, they would sprinkle seawater in every corner of every room in their house. Even the fire in the fireplace is sprinkled with water. Seaweed is dried and draped around doors, this is said to keep misfortune away.

A special protection was believed to be a "shark's egg". In the early days, they were called "purse of a mermaid", because of the special shape of the strings that were hanging on them in shape of purse handles.

Then the journey starts, but not without good luck charms. In Europe, the captain and crews paid large sums of money to get, what was called a "hood of fortune". That was the thin skin of the amniotic sac, which is around some babies heads when they are born. These children were believed to be blessed with luck and this quality should spread to his owner.

Besides that, this skin keeps the baby from drowning in the amniotic fluid, in the same way people believed, that it would also keep them from drowning. Since most of the witches were also midwives and had the chance, one time or another, to get one of these skins and to sell it to the seafarers.

Magicians didn't have to travel to faraway countries to find specially energized items, like the legendary "Sea bean", which was often found, washed up on the shores of England and Scotland by the Gulf Stream from America.

This bean is about as big as a chestnut and is the seed from the Macuna plant, which grows in the rainforests. Worn on a leather bracelet it would make a journey successful and bring riches to the bearer. If you, dear reader, should ever find an item like that while strolling along the shore, have a closer look and see, if it has a black rim around it, because these sea beans are believed to be very powerful!

Fishermen have a custom to make the Gods of the sea friendly. To see if they are in favour of the fishing, they took a piece of cork which was fixed to the net, cut a little slot into it and put in a silver coin. Then the net was cast into the water and they looked if the coin fell to the ground. If so, the fishermen knew that the "deal" was on. If this was not the case, they drilled a hole into the coin, because it meant bad luck for the one that spends it.

After a while they would repeat the procedure, and if the spirits of the sea would accept it, then fishing would be a success.

On all these boats was white magic a must.

Shrimp fishers bought from witches, a special kind of magic to assure a good haul. They took one of the clamps, opened it and put little pieces of paper with spells on them and mysterious wax mixtures into it. A silver cap and hot wax was used to seal it.

After that the "magic clamp" was hung up in the sailor's cabin. Some fishermen report, that there was never again an empty net.

A very special kind of power is given to the fossilized sea urchin. Most of these fossilized sea inhabitants had a five ray star on their back in the shape of the well-known pentagram and that protects against negative energies.

In the olden days and even today, in spite of motorisation, wind was and is a very important factor and witches were real experts on that. They can make the wind appear by calling it. Now you are asking: "How does that work please"? Nothing is easier than that!

Among several others there are two very popular ones. Witches work with Witchwoods or Witchstones. These are specially formed pieces of wood on a string, which were turned above the head on a long arm. Depending on the speed it was turned, it would make a hissing sound.

At a certain frequency, it would attract the spirits of the wind. Therefore many captains asked wise women for help, if there was no wind to leave the harbour.

But what is to do, when a sailboat was out in the middle of the sea and no witch was in sight? There was a solution even for that.

In the harbours you could and still can today, buy certain magic knots, which can attract the wind as well as calm it down. With quite some effort they made a ritual and tightened three knots in a rope together with the feathers from a seagull.

This kind of rope they could buy and take it along on the journey. If need be, one of the knots was untied and the wind could be called.

In the year 1616 Alexander Roberts wrote in his book " A Treatise of Witchcraft", that they had, by loosening one knot, a wind lasting 20 days, that took them to trade cities in Finland, Denmark, Lapland, Norway and other countries.

When they opened the second knot suddenly a storm appeared. During that storm the third knot loosened and a thunderstorm broke loose, so extreme, that no one dared to stick their head out of the window.

This magic has been so successful for centuries that it is watched over, that no one loosens one knot too much. You can see these ropes with knots in it on various ships and fishing boats today.

 The most of joy for a seafarer is, when he can arrive safely in the harbour, and when he can see the lantern, which his wife has put up symbolically.

This lantern is never to be blown out, because on account of the old superstition it ensures the safe return of her husband.

Dear readers, if you decide to spend your holiday at the sea, take a long walk down along the beach and maybe with a little bit of luck you will find a seabean or fossil sea urchin as good luck charm.

Protection magic and how to attract success

How to attract success and ward off the evil eye with a salt pouch

Do you know that you will find one of the oldest and most effective magic items in your kitchen? Salt plays an important role in a magic ritual. It can bring happiness and good luck and can keep the negative energies away. Numerous rituals have been passed on by word of mouth for many centuries and - they still exist!

When you move into a new home, bread and salt will be given to you, two essential parts of daily life.

The "white gold" is also a symbol of the power of life, vitality and energy. Protecting circles will be marked and places will be cleaned using salt before starting a ritual.

Salt is also an indicator for oracles. On special holidays, particularly during the "Holy Night", a small heap of salt put on a plate will tell you if the new year will be a good or a bad one. If the salt has not lost its shape in the morning, it will be a year with positive aspects. If, however, the salt is spread out on the plate, some problems will have to be solved during the next year.

A small bag of salt which you can carry with you is said to attract good luck and success.

If you are planning a trip, just throw a pinch of salt three times over your left shoulder and it will block negative energies which might follow you. Even actors throw a pinch of salt on the floor of the stage in order to guarantee the success of a performance.

Salt can also help in daily business life. Is there bullying in your company? Just draw a circle of salt around your workplace. That will create an energetic shield.

If you want to remove negative energies from rooms, take a little ceramic or china bowl of the size of a dessert plate, fill it with half a packet of simple salt, put seven copper coins on top and fill the bowl with water up to the rim. Now put this bowl at a place where you spend most of your time and leave it there.

It is physically normal that the water evaporates and a thin layer of salt sticks to the rim of the bowl. If, however, there are negative energies to be transformed, the water will become slimy in a short time and the salt will spread over the rim.

After the water has completely evaporated, clean the bowl and fill in new salt. That old alchemistic "air-condition" will help you in a wonderful way to clean rooms from negative energies.

Items for magic rituals or healing stones should be washed with salt water after each ritual. Always keep sufficient quantities of salt in stock because according to an old belief, running out of salt will attract bad luck. In the following, I will tell you a secret how you can benefit from the power of salt.

You need:

- 1 small green bag
- salt
- 3 copper coins
- 3 bay leaves
- 1 small pyrite (fool's gold)
- 1 white candle
- incense (e.g. "Olibanum")
- a small censer
- and charcoal

Start your magic ritual on a Tuesday evening. Create a harmonious atmosphere and first light the candle using a match. Light the charcoal and when it is glowing, put the incense on top. Now it's getting magic and thrilling! Take the little bag and say the following spell:

"Come to me, elements,

and be at my side,

assist me doing my ritual,

let it be successful and right!

I put three green bay leaves

into this bag.

I know that they are symbols

of glory and success.

They shall lead me on my way,

so that I do it all right,

the copper coins shall attract

much money and pride.

I now add the salt,

fill the bag almost completely,

this shall bring me good luck

and also protect me.

The small golden stone

will now make it perfect.

real magic witchcraft

is now in this bag."

So be it, so be it, so be it!"

Tie the little bag. If you want, you can seal it with wax. From now on, always carry this little charm bag with you! Do not talk about it. This is your little secret of success!

May this little ritual of white magic bring good luck, happiness and peace to you as soon as possible!

Magic besom

Have you ever seen a witch flying on her magical broom? If not I don't wonder why, because this is only an old fairytale! A besom is a main ritual tool of the witches and it symbolizes the ancient bound between the goddess and god. In witchcraft magical besoms are made of special wood. The shaft is built out from Ash. This wood stands for protection and the connection between heaven and earth. From Norse mythology the famous "Yggdrasil", the Ash tree, also called the "World Tree", is the greatest symbol of the connection to the Universe.

This wood represents the element ether and it reigns over the other four elements- earth, fire, water and air. The Birch is a tree which can clean and protect the Aura, houses and places. Twigs of the birch tree are need for the bristles. Last but not least the most popular item to make besoms for white magic is the willow tree!

Since thousands of years a lot of rituals and tales surround this mystical home of spirits. A willow tree grows mostly nearby the water and it shows people always water adders in nature too. Willow strands are needed for binding the birch twigs as bristles at the end of the shaft. Witches knew also the medical effect of a Willow tree because from its bark one of the most triumphant medicine is made- Salicylic acid better known as Aspirin®. It is helpful against fever, rheumatism and pain relieving.

Most enchanted besoms are decorated with secret signs. A sigil- a magical seal- is the personal touch of every magician. No one else can read it and only the owner of the besom knows its meaning. An also very often used besom is called Cinnamon broom. Cinnamon is said to clean people or places from negative energies and also protect houses against all evil. Traditionally manufactured from old woman, they are very powerful and can call good spirits into the home.

As you can read a magic besom is a powerful tool to clean and protect magical circles. It sweeps out all evil and is also a secret sign! If you place the broom outside your house, next to the main entrance other witches can see that a white witch is living here. The besom should always stand on the shaft pointing the bristles upwards! Only this way, it can work pretty well as a protective tool for your house! It is a luck bringing item now!

There are a lot of old customs all around the world about the power of magical besoms. One of the most popular traditions in folklore is seen on wedding days. The young couple is forced to jump over a besom to guarantee fertility, longevity and love. It is the commitment of caring for each other as long as they can.

Often decorated with flowers and colorful ribbons this wedding besoms show the importance of this superstition believes. If one day this couple wants to divorce their promise to each other, they have to jump backwards over the besom to break this commitment they have given.

If you want to have a magical besom too, you will need:

- 1 Ash stick
- Birch twigs
- Thin strands of the Willow tree
- Water, 1 big bowl, salt
- Scissor or sharp knife

First you have to fill the bowl full with water. Then put 3 Teaspoons full of salt in the bowl. Place the strands in it overnight. They will get more pliable then. Start with this white magic ritual to prepare the besom on a full moon night. Take the Ash stick and bind the birch twigs with the willow strands at the end of the broomstick. Be sure to bind it very strong at the shaft. When you have finished your work speak the following spell:

"Magical besom be at my side,

keep away evil and fill all with light!

Willow, Ash and Birch let grow,

my magical power wherever I go!

For sweeping the circle,

I consecrate you,

besom of witchcraft,

my enchanted tool.

From now and forever be at my side,

besom of mine in this magical night!

So shall it be!"

Your enchanted besom is ready to be used now! You will need it for several white magic rituals. It cleans the energy in your rooms! With this powerful tool you can also cast the magical circle! In times when you don't need it, place it with the bristles upwards nearby the entrance and it will keep away all evil! Please don`t use it as a daily household article. In modern times it is better to clean up the house with a vacuum cleaner! A magical besom should be only used for ritual work!

May your new enchanted besom always protect you and your house!

Witchbottles

In white magic it is well known to protect houses against all evil with a powerful witch bottle. This tradition has its origins in the United Kingdom. Most of the old bottles have been manufactured in 15th and 16th century.

Glass has been very rare and expensive in these times. The witches used for their magical bottles earthenware from Germany! These dark brown bottles were decorated with the portrait of Cardinal Robert Bellamin. He looked a little bit like the famous wizard Merlin from the legend of King Arthur. Bellamin is said to write magic spell books and has also been very interested in Astronomy.

This was very dangerous in times of the Inquisition! Because of his old face with a long, impressive beard the bottles were called "Bartmann", which means in the English language "Bearded man".

Another theory why those bottles where used for witchcraft rituals has been the story of the Greenman. In witches believe the Greenman is the God of nature and his portrait looks a little bit like the relief on the Bartmann bottle.

So I think, it is difficult to say which story tells the truth, but the mystical face on those bottles has been the reason why they have been used for the magical work.

Many witch bottles have been found all over Great Britain till today! Mostly when an old house has been demolished for building a new one, the workers found those bottles.

They have been placed in walls, buried in the garden or have been hidden nearby windows or doors. Some of them have been completely conserved and scientists could make investigations about the ingredients.

I think in our times this listing of ingredients sounds really creepy. Creating a classic "Witch Bottle" sounds a little absurd for uninitiated people. Urine, metal nails, usually beaten and crooked, glass or mirror shards, nails, pieces of leather and labeled in different ways, are just some of the most common utensils. To avert negative influences these ingredients also make sense!

If you want to make your own witch bottle, you don`t have to use urine! Modern witches can take symbolically cider vinegar! It will work as well!

If you want to create your own enchanted bottle you will need:

- 1 small bottle made out from glass or earthenware
- 6 iron or steel nails
- Cider vinegar
- 3 little mirror pieces (1cmx1cm)
- Black or blue wax
- 1 white candle/ candleholder/ matches
- Twine
- Golden glitter
- Something from your own body for example hairs

Start with your white magic ritual in a full moon night. Create a calm atmosphere. Light a white candle and visualize your desire.

After this take the bottle and fill in the nails. Traditionally the nails should be crooked to transform bad energies symbolically in good ones. Now add the small mirror pieces too.

Make 7 knots in the twine and put it in the bottle. Take a dash from the glitter and let it slowly pour like sand in your magic bottle. At least fill in the hairs and the cider vinegar.

I have deliberately given the cider vinegar instead of urine, so that the ritual is not too unhygienic. Vinegar also has a cleansing effect and certainly fulfills the same purpose. Hair and nails are also included as an information carrier!

Now seal the bottle with the heated blue or black wax. If you like, you can carve a Pentacle with a toothpick or twig in the warm wax.

A pentacle is the highest sign of the elements and it will keep your magic item protected.

Now it is getting exiting! Carry your witch bottle carefully outside into your garden. Hold the bottle in both hands and speak the following spell:

"May this bottle keep away all evil from this house and the humans which are living at this place! So shall it be!"

Now find a suitable place and make sure, that nobody else will dig in this special place where you put your witch bottle. Just dig it in deep enough, so it will not be found by other people.

Bury the bottle upside down in your garden. This way it will symbolically turn bad energies "upside down" into good energies! It means also the magic will never escape (witches logic is sometimes a little tricky). If you don`t live in a house, it is also allowed to take a big flower pot and dig it in. Then place it nearby the front door.

The witchcraft will work immediately! Just check it out!

Cats in white magic and how to protect them against bad energies

Why do witches always have a black cat as her pet? Maybe you will ask me why they have a black cat and not a black dog. I will explain it to you! There are a lot of superstitions around this beautiful little "tigers". Since ancient times there are a lot of myths and customs all over the world about these nocturnal creatures.

Thousands of years ago the Egyptians associated black cats with the goddess Bastet. As the moon goddess of the night, she was the guardian for houses and people. She is one of the most important deities of the ancient Egypt and represents fertility, love and joy.

In these times it was absolute crime to kill a cat and the murder of a cat was punished by death.

No house nearby the river Nil wanted to be without a cat! A minimum of one little living goddess on earth lived in every household. Numerous Cat mummies have been discovered. Archeologist explained, that they have also found little parcels filled with mice and goodies for the long journey to the cat`s afterlife. When a cat died the Egypt shaved their eyebrows as a sign of grief. This shows how important cats have been in the ancient Egypt.

Even in India cats are highly honored! The goddess of the woman and fertility is named Sasti. She is a beautiful cat and it is a sacred duty to feed the cats nearby the house every day.

In China cats lived like little princesses and prince at the royal palace. They are said to bring luck, success and happiness. Cats got famous for it and this way, it took only a short time till they got this popularity in Japan too. One reason was the ability to protect the precious silkworm cocoons against thousands of mice.

Another reason is that Chinese people see a cat as a good luck charm to protect the house against all evil. Today cats made out from pottery or porcelain can be seen in every Chinese shop almost in front of them or in the window to attract customers and for making many good deals. These always waving cats are called "Maneki Neko".

Originally cats had a good reputation as rat and mice hunters all over Europe as suddenly the Christian Church demonized cats as an incarnation of the devil. Their dark coat and the ability to see also in the night time have been the argument of the Church to see them as the "Prince of darkness".

Immediately the Pope issued a decree, that everyone who is friendly to a cat or feeds a black cat is also a friend of the devil! The Catholic Church told their followers, that witches can turn into a black cat, or black cats can turn into a witch!

This is absolutely nonsense! Countless human and animals have been demonized and murdered only because of this decree! In times of the Black death- the pestilence thousands of cats were killed. This has been a big mistake because the virus has been transmitted by rats and mice!

The big epidemic plague could grow more and more...Suddenly a lot of people became angry of the pope`s decree and started a revolution against this law! Very slowly people decided to hold the little tigers in their houses und human and animal could live a peaceful life in harmony again.

Witches use the special senses of the cats for several purposes. For example cats are able to detect earth radiation or water lines! Furthermore cats feel if a human is ill, or has fever. The person who is ill will feel relieve as soon as the cat is nearby him. They are said to take the pain and illness away!

The cat will not get ill either, because they transform these energies directly into the earth. Cats are also fantastic oracles!

An old custom explains it like this: If a cat licks its paws and coat, very soon guests will come into the house. If you have a question which can be answered with "Yes" or "No" just have a look about your cat! If it enters the room with its left paw it is a "Yes"! If it taps with her right paw over the threshold it means a "No"!

Cats can do the weather forecast too! Whenever you want to know if sunshine or rain is coming up just ask your cat! If your pet licks its fur against the growth it will be raining.

Please close your door and windows if the cat is brushing its fur along the furniture! This means a storm is coming up and if the cat doesn't want to go outside- the answer is really easy- it is getting bitter cold!

As you can see - a black cat belongs to superstition and witchcraft and this little tiger is very helpful in our life! If you want to protect your pet against all evil then write beneath the water bowl the following spell:

"Holy Bastet daughter of the moon,

Let my cat always come home very soon.

Protect it with your guiding light,

Also when it hunts in darkest nights!

Please give good energy and happiness on all ways of live,

I am begging you holy Bastet please stay at its side!

So be it, so be it, so be it!"

Every day when your cat is drinking its water, it will also be blessed by the old Egyptian goddess!

I wish your cat a long and pleasant live. May the stars light always the nocturne ways of your little Tiger!

The witches spell book

A witch without her magical spell book is like a car without a steering wheel. You wonder why? I will explain it to you! The "Book of Shadows" or also called "Grimoire"is like an instruction manual. It contains how to use the magic utensils, herbs, spells and potions.

Without this enchanted book rituals would be only work uncontrolled like the car without the steering wheel. That means magic/car would turn into somewhere and only by a lot of fortunate the wishes will really be fulfilled.

Therefore a detailed instruction is extremely important to cause positive and helpful results.

That is the reason why witches write all their recipes and spells in a spell book. It is a little bit like a kind of a diary, because only this way a white witch can check out if her rituals have worked as well!

Some very old spell books got really famous! In earlier times they were not made out from paper. The ancient Greeks scratched their spells on rolled lead sheets to protect houses against the evil eye. They had the old knowledge and wisdom to speak different mantras to their deities. To attract love, luck, success or health they used those old spells.

In Egypt, the "Papyri Graecae Magicae" is one of the famous old magician documents, because it is a "community work" as a result of Egyptian, Greek and Jewish magic. The most famous part of this papyrus has been written by Moses himself and explains how to use secret codes to get in contact with the angels. In the year 1462 Italian Cosimo di Medici discovered a spell book from the ancient Greeks called" Hermes Trismegistos".

He was very surprised and interested in this powerful old magic and suddenly magic work got a new Renaissance all over Europe. In the Middle Ages spell books have been very modern. Every Alchemist, Magician or witch wrote her own book of shadows. For example the "Key of Solomon" has been copied a thousand of times.

Unfortunately the version changed from copy to copy, that nothing today can be seen from the original text. John Dee- the astrologer and magician of the Royal family in 16th century realized this wrong copies and translation errors. He corrected them and it is amazing that all the old instructions started to work! This book is still to be seen in the British Museum in London.

But even in Germany spell books had a big boom in this time. Agrippa von Nettesheim – Alchemist, Magician and Physician, who lived in Cologne, wrote a special book about magic.

It took him 23 years to finish his almagest. "De occulta philosophia" is one of the biggest text books in magic and it is still used from generations of magicians till today. At that time it was incredibly dangerous to write such almagests, because the Inquisition was always present.

Agrippa of Nettesheim defended his, as he called it "Holy Magic" and the Catholic Church couldn't do anything against it. Similar to the famous Nostradamus he used his medical knowledge of herbs to fight against the pestilence. Not infrequently, he could heal some people from this terrible disease by using his magical healing knowledge! Revolutionary in those times!

Even today, his book is one of the most competent magical writings and the basics for many rituals! For several centuries Germany has been a veritable "Paradise" of magic spell books. Abraham of Worms describes how even in the middle of summer snow, ice and hail can be summoned and many stories of him are describing that he really got these skills!

In the middle of the 19th century a historian found some very important spells. Beneath the Cathedral of Merseburg the manuscripts have been undiscovered for 1000 years. That is the reason why today they are called the "Merseburg incantations". These incantations are describing for example how to heal broken bones. Also spells how to help animals by using the power of magic were included.

Many of the old magic books also refer to the pagan believe, as well as to the Christian saints. Hundreds of years ago books have been written and painted by hand.

A century ago the antiquary Michael Voynich discovered an ancient manuscript from the 13th century. In a sophisticated coding system there are shown a lot of astronomical, anatomical, and herbal recipes .Till today no person has been able to encrypt these complex secret codes.In our modern times, most of the spell books are written in a style we are able to understand. So a lot of people suddenly got an access to this old knowledge.

It took time to explain, that this old spells can only work in accordance to the cosmic laws! Only this way, rituals are helpful and working in a white magic way! In Great Britain it was Gerald Gardner, who wrote several books and became a very popular expert in the history of white magic. Even today, many rituals are based on his recipes!

I am always searching for old magic formulas and sometimes I have found very curios ones that make me smile. For example, the 400 years old ritual to find a lot of gold! The spell describes, that gold can only be found by black chickens. If this would be true, I think that a lot of people would have black chickens! This is absolutely nonsense! The poor little chicken won`t find any gold!

If you want to write your own Grimoire, many materials are allowed. It is not important if it is a simple ring- binder or a very expensive book made out of luxurious leather.

It should be able to take up many pages so that there is enough space for a lot of spells, notes and recipes. A spell book will be a companion for life, because it is the only way to proof the results permanently! If you are wise enough write your spells down for the next generation. Believe me they will be absolute grateful for this spell book.

May light full spells always accompany you!

Hagstones for wishes and weather

Have you ever heard about the magical Hagstones? I will show you how to use them in white magic rituals! Hagstones or also called WItchstones can be found at the Mountains, a river or at the ocean side. These are stones with one or more holes in the middle. These mystical stones can also look like animal or human heads.

Millions of years the Element water has constantly hollowed out the hard material. This shows the strong power of water! Depending on where they are found, it is referred to these rare pieces of nature, a force corresponding to the location. For example a Hagstone is found nearby a river is said to clear thoughts and situations. Witchstones who came from a mountain area can be an energetic help in self-realization rituals.

Therefore, it is not surprising that this magical utensil is used for various occasions and in other parts of the world too! In Europe they are also often referred to as "wishing stones", or "sacred stones". In Germany there are still some farmers who practice the old tradition to pour the milk from cows through a large Hagstone so that it cannot clot during a thunderstorm!

A Witchstone placed over a barn door keeps away all evil from the cattle. Worn around the neck on a ribbon, very small Hagstones are powerful good luck charms! Even in earlier times it was believed that such a stone set under the bed, could ward off diabolical nightmares and attacks during the night. It stabilizes your good night sleep! Centuries ago there has been an old custom in Scandinavia to pour beer through the hole in the witch-stone on the belly of pregnant women, to facilitate childbirth. Well, this is all a long time ago and today the modern medicine is the better way to support a birth process!

In Saudi Arabia the power of the sacred stones is also known. Camel drivers bind these perforated stones, which can be found in the desert, around young Camels neck to protect them against the "evil eye".

In many parts of the UK fishermen knot Hagstones on the bow of their ships to safely navigate through the stormy sea. Very interesting has been the mentally effect when in the middle age it was popular to give a Witchstone to a person at court. The defendant had to hold the Stone in his hand and the judge could be sure that he was telling the truth meanwhile a judicial inquiry. The fear of the defendant has been so great that he could be unmasked by the magical stone that he told the truth.

In Witchcraft the mystical Hagstones can do much more! The stones are said to be an ancient "Mobile phone" to the world of fairies, elves and other spirits of the nature. The communication with the spirits is very important for white magic!

Whenever a white Witch is making a ritual, she calls the good spirits and the elements for supporting her work. With a Hagstone a witch is also able to call wind, sun and rain! For this purpose, a thin rope or a cord is threaded through the hole in the stone and firmly attached to multiple nodes. At a free place in nature the magical tool is taken and swing arm`s lengths in circles above the head. Parallel to this old magical spells are spoken. There are even witches who specialized in these rituals! Mostly these witches are called by farmers in times of drought to call the rain for their fields.

Other people ask the wise woman for calling sunshine weather. For example prior to major festivals and events that takes place under the open sky. Wedding couples also seek the advice of the stones vibrating magic, to be blessed and married under a blue and sunny sky! In the United Kingdom there can be a completely different weather situation at a square from only one mile! Four seasons in just one day! With a smile on their face the old people use to say: "Too many "Weather witches" are very active today!"

If you are on holiday and the weather is bad, just watch out for magical Hagstones! If you have found one, you can make a powerful white magic ritual to make your wishes or a day full of sunshine come true! The easiest way is if you take the Hagstone in your left hand and visualize your desire. Then use the thumb of your right hand to circle clockwise on the top of the stone. The request should be repeated each "round" whilst doing the circles on the Hagstone. At least nine times! Witches use to cast the magical spells the whole night long to give them a lot of magic power! It is usual they have repeated the magical phrase until dawn for hundreds of times!

You can also use the wonderful Stones in another magical way- red cords or ribbons thread through the hole for three times, whilst casting your wish, will manifest your good intentions! The number three plays an important role in magical work, because it symbolizes the Holy Trinity and the fulfillment by magical wishes. So if you have the good fortune to find a stone with several holes it can help you to make your wish come true!

Keep the Hagstone hidden at a secret place! Don't tell other people about your little secret! Speech is silver, silence is golden! This is important for a fast working Witchstone magic! If the enchanted stone is not so big, you can wear it also as a pendant on a cord.

So if you are on holiday watch out for the mystical Hagstones! The wonderful gifts of Mother Nature will help you making wishes and always sunny days come true!

A ritual for Demeter

Autumn is the most magical season of the year! Mother Nature shows her beautiful face with trees and their leaves in brown, red and golden colors. It is the time to be thankful for the gifts of the harvest. Hazelnuts, Apples, Grapes, Grain and much more fills our table for the wintertime. It is also the time for saying "Thank you" to the goddess of autumn.

The best known of the harvest mythologies is the story of the virgin Persephone and her beautiful mother Demeter. One day Persephone has been captured by the God of the underworld called Hades. For a long time no one knew where Persephone had gone. Demeter has been very sad and so she decided to let the nature sleep for six month.

In earlier times there have been only two seasons in one year. The light full time called summer and the dark season called winter. Zeus has seen the great sorrow of his wife Demeter and sent Hermes to persuade Hades to release his beautiful daughter. Hades, the God of the Darkness, created a plan to keep Persephone in his Kingdom. He gave the beautiful maiden six Pomegranate seeds. If a person who enters the Underworld eats something in the dark caves, he will never return to the land of the living!

Persephone was hungry and so she ate the red tasty seeds. The Pomegranate had been enchanted and so she had to marry Hades. Finally she could escape from her husband, but she had to promise, to come back after six month. This way, every year she can bring brightness, light and love to the lost souls of the eternity. In summertime Persephone spends six month with her mother Demeter and together they grow all plants on earth. From the autumn equinox on 21th of September to Easter she returns to her husband spending the next six month together.

From this old Greek mythology, the pagan believe honors Demeter for her great work. That is the reason why she is the Goddess of the harvest and grain! In autumn white witches celebrate several rituals of thankfulness to Demeter. If you, dear readers want to celebrate a white magic ritual in honor to Demeter too you can decorate your witches' altar with grain, sunflowers, apples, grapes, hazelnuts, corn and straw. Let your creativity run wild!

Place some yellow, brown and green candles on the table too and light them with a match. A traditionally Demeter altar includes also fresh baked bread and some fruit juice. If you want, you can invite friends and family to your little white magic ritual.

It is much nicer to celebrate this ritual of thankfulness together with people you love! Start with this ritual on sunny and warm Sunday morning. When all guests have arrived at your home welcome them and ask them to hold each other's hand.

Now speak the following spell:

"Demeter we all are very thankful for your great gift of the harvest! Now we have strength for the coming winter! Let us hold on to each other for the times, when we all need a helping hand. And also let us stay together when times are plentiful! Let us stay together also when life is wonderful! We hail also your daughter Persephone, who brings so much light into the darkness! Thank you for all you have done for humankind since thousands of years! "

Now take the bread and give a little piece to every guest. Everyone should feed each other with this blessed bread. It symbolizes the solidarity of your family and friends. Demeter bread is filled with abundant energy! After this have a wonderful evening together with your guests! In ancient times everything has been allowed! Dancing, singing, laughing- just having fun with thankfulness to the ancient Greek Demeter - the goddess of the harvest!

Samhain (Halloween) and a traditional Barmbrack

On October 31st is Halloween and I would like to tell you about some of the customs and rituals that go along with that day. Witches call this day Samhain and it has a Celtic origin. It all started about 5000 years ago in Ireland. The meaning of the word Samhain is "end of summer".

Samhain is a celebration of the dead. In this night the veil between the worlds is very thin, that is why the spirits and other creatures can easily come into our world. That is the reason why the people prepared food for the "visitors". They wanted to worship the dead and tried to keep them away from doing any damage to the house and the inhabitants. One thing was for sure; they didn't want any contact between the living and the dead, so in spite of the holy day they went to bed early and left the rooms to the "visitors". So who ever heard a noise better didn't bother to look for it, because to nosy ones could just disappear in the other world.

The Irish changed this custom a bit, by putting on some spooky costumes, so the dead and the spirits would pass them by and not recognize them as living people. Masks and costumes only meant to deter. That evening is especially suited for prophecy! Even today there are a lot of traditions to interpret the signs of the coming year. One of the most common ways is the baking of a cake and putting in a ring which is called "Barmbrack".

Ingredients:

- 500 gr. of flour
- 1 cup of milk
- 1 cube of yeast
- 1 egg
- 2 big spoons of butter
- 100 gr. of sugar
- 250 gr. of sultanas
- 125 gr. of currants
- 50 gr. of candied orange
- a dash of cinnamon powder
- icing sugar

First take the flour, milk, butter, egg, yeast and sugar. Knead all ingredients and let it rest for about 20 minutes. Add the sultanas, currants, the candied orange and the cinnamon to the dough. Now comes the most important thing- the golden ring! Put it in the dough too! Bake the cake for half an hour at 220 degrees C and after the cake is cooled down, you can put the icing sugar on it. Whoever finds the ring, will have a partner to be going steady with the next year.

You can also use this ritual for financial success or a child wish. Accordingly there are different symbolic items to put into the cake. For example a golden coin or a bean.

The word "Halloween" is of American origin. It was created by Irish immigrants and formerly meant "all hallows eve(ning)". In the process of Christianization dignitaries used some clever methods to integrate the Christian holidays into the heathen holidays, so that the people didn't had to change their habits.

There are many myths and stories about Halloween. One of the most well-known is the **Irish story of Jack O' Lantern**.

Once upon a time there lived a very mean old man by the name of Jack. As the day came, when he should pass over to eternity, the angels denied him his entry to heaven because of his vicious way of life. So down he went to hell to enter there, but even the devil didn't want this insidious, underhanded guy and gave Jack a burning piece of coal in his hand to deter him.

Jack left and took a turnip from the field and hollowed it out in order to put the coal inside it to get a lantern for his dark and restless search for his last place of rest. Since this time Jack O' Lantern spooks around through the night of Halloween. On account of this nice and yet terrible story arouse the custom to hollow out a pumpkin and carve a grimace in it to deter bad spirits. In America they meanwhile have big competitions in "Pumpkin Carving".

So all over the world people offer sweets to the dead, in order to prevent damage to the house and that the dead would leave as quick as possible. Poor people in those days used this ritual and dressed up like ghosts in order to steal the food which was offered. As time went on, children and youths took over the story and made up the speech "Trick or Treat". Kids just love to dress up in spooky costumes. They go on through the night from house to house and if somebody doesn't give them any treats, they play little tricks on them.

I recommend that you decorate your altar on Samhain with some apples, twigs of hazelnut and corn as well as a cross made of evergreen, vermouth, yew tree, grain, chrysanthemums, nuts etc. Bind it and lay it on the altar. This will also protect your house!

Put 4 brown and 3 yellow candles, which you consecrated before with carnation oil, also on it. Brown is the color of the earth element and yellow the golden sunlight. Together they symbolize the colors of autumn.

The use of joss sticks is a necessity on this night. A mixture of incense made out of myrrh, bay leaf, thyme, vermouth, chamomile and rose blossoms is useful.

This night is ideal to say goodbye to the summer and to get into the mood for the more dark and contemplative time of the year. It is also the time of letting go and cleaning.

Write down on small piece of paper all the things you want to get rid of and offer it to the cleansing power of the fire. Invite friends for this special evening, because this is a perfect night for divination.

Maybe you want to put a pumpkin and something to eat in front of your doorstep, to deter Jack O' Lantern and to be friendly to your ancestors. I wish you an enchanting Halloween!

Yuletide customs

Mistletoe magic

Have you ever thought about the wonderful white magic when you kiss your beloved partner underneath a mistletoe? If not- let me explain it to you! There are a lot of myths surrounding this magical plant. Mistletoe has its origins from the old English word "Misseltan," which means "missel twig". The Latin name is Viscum album. It is the European type of mistletoe. It is a green shrub with small, yellow flowers and white, sticky berries.

Like other evergreens, the Mistletoe is a symbol of immortality. From early times, mistletoe has been regarded as one of the most magical, mysterious and sacred plants of folklore customs.

The tradition of kissing under the mistletoe is said to be associated with the Greek festival of Saturnalia. The use of mistletoe was found in the ancient marriage rites, as it was believed that mistletoe had the power to confer fertility!

Another belief connected with mistletoe was that it possessed 'life-giving' powers. According to a northern mythology, it is told that a Mistletoe restored Balder, son of the Goddess Freya, to life.

Ancient Celts believed the mistletoe was full of miraculous healing and strong benevolent powers. In the medieval Germany, the plant was called "Allheil" what means "allhealing" and used medicinally for a variety of ailments. Druids considered mistletoe as a holy plant that protects against all evil spirits and had great medicinal value. A tree that hosted a mistletoe plant was sacred by the gods.

The most powerful mistletoe, of course, grew on the sacred oak. Druids celebrated a five days ritual after the winter solstice to lose Mistletoe from oaks. The 21st December, also called Yul, is the time of the winter solstice, and plays a major role in the witch festivals.

Yul is the beginning of the annual cycle in the Pagan and is due to the fact that this day is the longest night of the year is especially important. It represents the rebirth of the light, as from this date, the following days are getting longer and the light begins to rule over the dark. At this time Druids took a golden sickle to cut mistletoe from the tree. The sprigs should never touch the earth!

That is the reason why another priest has held his robe like a net to catch the falling mistletoe! It was wrapped in a clean white cloth and the Druids went from house to house for bringing a twig to the families to protect them from all evil. It was hung up over the front door case so that every guest or family member, who entered the house, had to walk underneath it.

This is the original tradition that still holds in the modern day to use Mistletoe for the adorning of houses at Christmastime!

Later in the 18th century the simple sprigs of mistletoe were replaced by a kissing ball. This is a ball made out from different flowers, herbs and also mistletoes. Every single who kisses an unmarried person underneath this ball will get married within one year! It is no mystery to me why those Kissing balls are highly frequented on Wedding Days!

Another superstition belief is to put a twig of mistletoe under the pillow before they go to sleep. The magical plant will reveal what their bridegroom will look like!

The correct mistletoe ritual would be for the man to remove one berry when he kisses a woman. Please wash your hands because the white berries are poisonous! When all the berries are gone, there is no more kissing underneath that plant.

If you dear readers want to use the magical power of mistletoes too, you can prepare a white magical gift for your friends and family too! You will need a red ribbon. Holly twigs, fir tree sprigs and mistletoe. Tie the red ribbon around the little bunches made from of this Yuletide plants.

Hold each one in your hands and close your eyes. Visualize a golden light flowing into every bunch, which then enlightens them. Bring these bunches to your friends and family. Tell them about the old traditions!

My guess would be that they all want to try it out! Especially to kiss a man or woman underneath the mistletoe!

A fir tree bouquet to protect a house

At Christmas time and anywhere people are walking from shop to shop buying Christmas presents for their beloved friends and family. There is a delicious smell in the air, because of the Christmas cookies baked with special spices. A lot of houses are decorated with thousands of lights bringing a special atmosphere in those dark nights of the winter.

But the absolutely Christmas superstar is the fir tree! Many people don't even know why it is being decorated with candies, red ribbons and crystal balls. Let's go back into past times to see where those traditions of the Christmas tree are coming from.

Old legends reportedly this tree in general is the carrier of the universe. In pre-Christian times, a fresh cut tree was brought into a house has been a sign of rebirth and renewal of all life. Mostly people choose a fir tree because this evergreen plant would defy most acts of nature.

In earlier times walnuts were placed in the tree as a symbol of fertility. Red ribbons have the same meaning, because the red color is also associated with the same meaning. Candies and sweets according to superstitions believe to have always food in the house throughout the year. In ancient times they didn't had crystal balls. Apples where hung up in the tree as a sign of the goddess.

In Great Britain that tree was called a bringer of light. By druids consecrated twigs were believed to be good luck charms and they were kept in the house for a whole year.

At the time of the winter solstice or at Christmas eve little twigs of evergreen where given to friends, but if one of them didn't get one, it meant bad luck for the next year, because negative spirits could enter the house very easily.

Even today we decorate our Christmas presents to someone we love with a twig of evergreen for protecting him against evil spirits.

In magic use we don't only associate the fir tree as a heathen symbol of return or rebirth. We also see the healing aspect! There are a lot of possibilities to use the ingredients of this tree for making a good medicine!

The active substance of the fir tree helps to cure bronchitis and asthma. Beer made from fir tree needles help to heal scurvy and this beer boiled, cool down and taking some sip can help to solve problems if someone is ill with bladder and kidneys disease.

One of the first chewing gum has been the resin from the fir tree. It helped to prevent soreness of the gums or even bacterial attack. The oil of the fir tree is good against muscle aches and neuralgia.

Therefore I will describe a little ritual for the Christmas season which can bring courage, hope, protection and confidence for the next year!

You will need:

- 3 twigs of fir tree
- 4 little twigs of boxwood
- 3 white Christmas candles and holders
- Red ribbon
- 12 walnuts
- Golden varnish
- Silver wire
- Hot Glue gun/ hot glue

On December 21st, at winter solstice, bind all the twigs together. Paint the walnuts with the golden lacquer. After that use the hot glue to attach a red ribbon to each nut and bind them to the twigs. Now light up the candles. Hold the arrangement of plants and nuts in your hands and give it a blessing with the following words:

"Holy tree I bless you as a sign of light!

Keep all evil away and protect this house!

Give joy to all human and pets

And let hope come into their life.

Twelve walnuts for each month,

Golden and bright, bring back the holy light!

Luck will always stay by my side,

With angel glow and heavens delight!

So mote it be!"

Place this magical fir tree bouquet near the front door to keep evil spirits away for the next twelve months.

Yuletide is the most suitable season for enjoy good old times. Give the fir tree tradition to your children and grandchildren to keep those old customs alive!

Dear readers, please try to buy a Christmas trees with roots! It is a much nicer if you can take it back into your garden or to the forest again! If we give something back to Mother Nature, Christmas becomes a feast for the family and the fir tree too!

The magical divination soup

Can you imagine that a delicious soup could be a divination tool? I'm not joking! Let me explain how to use it for telling you the future in the upcoming months!

Mostly people are starting the New Year with a lot of new year-resolutions. Some of them want to stop smoking, others try to lose weight and make more sports. Unfortunately, it is not so easy to implement all these good wishes. The white magic helps us to make wishes come true! Our mind is always faster than matter.

The more we think about an idea, the more we have to work to manifest it! We should internalize our wishes. How can that better be done, as with a magic soup!

Don't worry; you don't need any exotic ingredients like toads, spider legs or bats. Witches love all animals and we make our soups preferably with vegetables.

No animal should be killed for magical practices! It would be against the cosmic rules! The preparation of food is a ritual in its self and we can let a lot of positive energy flow into it! Let's see what we need! In ancient times, witches took a three-legged cauldron and placed it over the open fire.

In modern times we rather cook on an electric- or gas range and use a conventional cooking pot! To stir the soup use a wooden spoon, no metal please, because metal has a meaning in white magic and would adulterate the result. Start with this ritual in a new moon night!

For the recipe we need:

- Half a gallon of water
- 1 readymade vegetable soup
- 2 carrots
- 1 peace of celery
- 1 courgette
- 1 piece of leek
- 1 tomato and 1 teaspoon of tomato paste
- 1 onion
- Salt and pepper
- 3 eggs and a bunch of parsley

If you may think now: „Well that's nothing special!" - you're wrong! Magic works on the basics of analogy. The soup is made of water. Water is an element and a carrier of information. That means everything in this world made out of water can be magically programmed. Visualize your wishes while filling the pot with water.

Now put the pot onto the stove. The element fire is now added by the heat of the oven.

Let us go on with the vegetable. Cut the vegetables into slices. Slices are associated with coins and this means, to get a lot of money for the next months of this New Year!

Carrots grow in the underground and represent the earth element. Courgettes are a magical symbol of the air because they join heaven and earth. Leek is a secret sign to be recognized by and is since the Lord knows when, the sign of victory! We want to succeed with our new year a resolution.

That's the reason why we cook this soup. The Teutons held the leek holy and gave it the rune "Laukaz" in their alphabet. A really fabulous vegetable!

Now take the tomato and put it into the soup. For good reasons the Austrians call it "apple of paradise"! It is the fruit of love. To find a partner or to fasten a friendship the tomato is an important part of magic! Add the tomato-paste as well, because it has also the colour red- the colour of love.

The onion is a surely divine vegetable, because it has 7 mystic skins. It gives our ritual an energetic protection! In the Middle Ages people always carried an onion with them to be protected against all evil. Parsley is an aphrodisiac from Mother Nature.

Therefore it was always a part in flower bouquets of a bride. By the way- this plant is green and this is the colour of success. Celery brings us joy of life and gives strength to it all. Pepper gives us zest for life and salt cleans the soul.

Now let the soup simmer for 45 Minutes. Then stir the soup anti-clockwise for 9 times and speak the following spell:

"New year I welcome you,

please make my wishes all come true.

Money, luck and confidence,

a job and love and health as well,

this is my little witchcraft spell!

The air, the earth, the fire and water,

they guide me because I'm a goddess daughter!

This soup is sealed for 9 times now,

the universe will fore fill it somehow!

Oh great goddess please be at my side,

in and guide me in this magical night!

So shall it be!"

Now slowly add the stirred eggs to the soup. Make sure, that the soup doesn't boil anymore.

The egg is a symbol of the earth and fertility. The white of the egg and the yellow of the yolk represents the metals gold and silver. Did you ever think of that while eating your breakfast?

Now watch this: The egg poaches immediately and forms all kinds of figures. It's just like reading tealeaves. You can let your imagination run away with you.

Maybe you can see a heart. It shows you a good partnership. A house for example symbolizes security in your life.

Now the soup is ready to be eaten. Please see the whole thing still as a ritual, you have put many good thoughts and visions into it, let it now be internalized.

Enjoy your magic food! With every spoon you're eating please imagine how your wishes and resolutions are coming true! You will feel a strong energetic power after this mystic meal.

I wish you fulfillment in everything you want to achieve and may all your wishes come true!

The author

Susanne Klimt is a Clairvoyant, Tarot reader, White Witch and expert for paranormal phenomenon. She has written numerous books and publications in European journals about white magic, ancient mystical places and traditions from all over the world.

Susanne Klimt keeps old customs alive and with her seminaries in Germany and the United Kingdom she shows people how to live a happy and peaceful life. Since years Susanne Klimt is also a TV presenter and has been in many TV shows in Germany, Switzerland and Austria.

She is an well known artist too. Susanne Klimt has drawn her own Fortune telling cards. She also loves to create paintings about Scottish landscapes. As a light worker she is a keeper of the old healing knowledge. Since over thirty five years she teaches people how to spell the old prayers for several purposes.
Her books are filled with wisdom, old customs and a very unique humor. Everything she does and creates is made for to bring back vitality, braveness and confidence.

Contact

www.art-and-more.co.uk